Imminent List Building

B. Vincent

Published by RWG Publishing, 2021.

IMMINENT LIST BUILDING

First edition. June 11, 2021.

Written by B. Vincent.

Also by B. Vincent

Affiliate Marketing
Affiliate Marketing

Standalone
Affiliate Recruiting
Business Layoffs & Firings
Business and Entrepreneur Guide
Business Remote Workforce
Career Transition
Project Management
Precision Targeting
Professional Development
Strategic Planning
Imminent List Building

Table of Contents

Imminent List Building

Hello and welcome to this course on Imminent List Building. In this course, we'll show you how to collect leads in the US, automatically, without your prospects needing to type anything, into a form. This course is divided into three modules. Module One gives you a brief overview of this new concept, module two covers the tool we'll be using, and how to set it up, and Module three goes over the unique follow-up campaigns you'll need. By the time this course is over, you'll know how to generate leads, automatically. So, without further ado, let's dive into the first module. Okay guys, welcome to module one. In this module, our expert will give you a brief intro to this new concept, so get ready to take some notes, and let's jump right in.

Module 1

Alright so let's talk about this interesting novel. And, frankly, totally unprecedented form of list building. There is a very high likelihood that you have not heard of this yet. It's new to the industry, relatively new to the industry. It is a form of lead generation and list building, that allows you to capture the email, the name, and even the physical mailing address, of visitors to your website, even if they didn't opt-in or tap on anything in your website.

And the way it does that is based on anonymous digital identifiers, of the people who visit your site, being matched against a giant database of real profiles, of people in the United States. Now, this is only in the United States, that this can be done, or rather the leads that you collect can only be in the United States. If you're outside the United States and you want to engage in this. It's obviously very important that you speak to your business lawyers, your attorneys, and in fact, that's always something to do anyway, even in the United States, but in the United States, we do have generally well-known CAN-SPAM laws. Okay, and this is 100% compliant with those, it's in compliance with the CAN-SPAM regulations, it's in compliance with CCPA, and with all of the applicable regulations and rules and laws that you can find in the United States. So, it's very, very

carefully crafted in a way that is totally legally legit, even if it sounds a little bit too good to be true.

Now what this capture is not every visitor. In fact, in many cases, it will be a minority. But according to this tool, they can actually typically match a 70% of the visitors that come to your website, to at least one, identifier in their database. The tool is called GetEmails, and it works by placing a pixel on your website, that grabs it, sees it analyzes and it grabs those anonymous digital identifiers, and it compares those identifiers of your visitors to their database. And if there's a match, it adds those people, their names, their emails, and your physical mailing address, to your list, to your list of leads. And if you're wondering, how do they do that legally, like I said it's all compliant with CCPA and CAN-SPAM ACT and all the rules and regulations, if you think about it today. A lot of people, a lot of people have opted in and click the Yes button on, you know agreements for things like Facebook or 1000 other websites that they use, in which they are allowed to, and by then, I mean the sites that they're agreeing that they're signing these agreements with, they're allowed to, import those identifiers into a database, okay. And the database is very large in the United States, it's very large. The database in question here is associated with around 250 million individuals in the US, according to this tool.

So, we have to acknowledge here that there is a basis for a discussion of ethics here. Many people think that something is not necessarily ethical, simply because it's legal. And that's true, this, however, would seem one could make the case, one could argue that it only rises to the level of potentially annoying people, that because it's all done correctly, in accordance with the applicable laws and regulations, and it's all based on consent

that people gave at some point, and so on and so forth, that there isn't really any significant concern with ethics, there is a concern however with annoyance, annoyance. And so, you have to be very careful with this if you're going to use this tool. And that's really going to come up in the follow-ups, that you're going to send these people after they've joined your list, based on those anonymous digital identifiers. And that's going to be covered in the final module, module number three.

But this tool is very effective, and it has very high-quality information, very high-quality leads that you're getting. They have very careful algorithms, in which they only pass on people who have been active within their network in their database within the last 14 days, and they also scrub it, for people who have been known to complain and unsubscribe a lot. Right, so you're really getting very high-quality, leads onto your list here. And they've proven that you can get some very good, and favorable opt-in rates and some surprisingly low complaint rates. Okay, there aren't going to be complaints, there's no question about it's a very novel concept than a novel method, and people are getting emails from you, that they really didn't consent to, at least not in the traditional sense. And so, there's going to be complaints, but they're surprisingly low, surprisingly low, and in fact, this tool claims that the complaint rates are less than point 1%, okay, which is again surprisingly low. They do a good job of scrubbing and cleaning like I mentioned, they do in fact, respect consumer privacy, because every person who is in this database have opted in, to the network or the database, at some point in the past, and they actually maintain records of the date in which they opted in, and the URL for it and all that good stuff.

Now a lot of people say well you know when people opt-in. Sometimes it's because they had a little, you know, legal pop up on their page that said I accept and they were lazy and they clicked I accept, and sure there's debate about that. And people are free to agree or disagree about the details and the ethics of it and so on and so forth. But the fact is it is completely legally compliant, and it is an option that you're certainly able to consider if you're doing business in the United States. Ultimately the benefit of doing this is that you're getting more emails, you're getting a way to contact people who have expressed some interest in your business because they came to your website.

And the vast majority of people who come to your website or to your web properties, your landing pages end up leaving, and they're gone forever, and you can contact them. Well, now a significant percentage of them can be contacted and GetEmails has indicated that that can actually translate into reclaiming 20% of your revenue, in some cases. So even in the case where you're only getting a minority of visitors who come to your site, who are able to be matched against this database and added to your email list. It's an incredible benefit because those are people who you can now reach out to, in an appropriate way. We'll talk about that in module three, but those are people who you can now reach out to who you otherwise would not have been able to reach out to and that translates to nothing but good news for your business. And so, this is a very cool tool again, there's plenty of room for debate and disagreement. Regarding the question of ethics and, you know, annoyance and so on and so forth. And then no one needs to use this tool, but it's an important one to know that it is out there. And I think the potential benefits, just in and of themselves, apart from everything else are pretty clear and that this is a tool, definitely worth looking into. And so, in the next module, we're actually going to go into the tool itself we're going to look at how to set it up, what to expect inside. How to paste the pixel on your website and how it all sort of functionally works, and then in the module after that, we'll look at the logic and the style of follow-up that you need to be using, because again this is a very unique situation. So, let's go ahead and move on to the next module.

Module 2

Hey folks, welcome to module two. In this module, our expert will cover the special tool we'll be using. So, get ready to take some notes, and let's jump right in.

Alright so here we are inside of the GetEmails account. This is the dashboard; all we're going to do in this module is click around and sort of look at how things work in here and how to navigate the site and ultimately get your pixel code and use the product by putting your pixel on your page. So, this is the dashboard, like I said you can actually see the chart that indicates you know, your contacts that were acquired over the course of a given period of time. This here is actually a launch period that we had in November, so we had a product launch where we had a whole bunch of sales coming in, we had a whole lot of people coming to our website, and well, as is usually the case the vast majority of them left without doing anything, then it's always going to be the case on a sales page or an opt-in page, most people are going to leave without doing anything, and this case we actually grabbed, a total of 728 of those contacts, which we otherwise would not have gotten they didn't opt in to an email list, and they didn't buy anything. But we do have the ability to reach out to them and send some type of communication to them, because it was grabbed here.

Now there is and they're showcasing it here there is an ability with GetEmails to track your revenues, and that is by placing certain codes, a more specialized code on the pages of your website and indicating what they represent in terms of, you know, a sale, you know, so the success page after purchasing, you know, a certain product that might be worth $30. Right, and so GetEmails knows that after it lands on that page, or in this case it actually integrates with Shopify, so it's probably much more streamlined than that but basically you can figure out based on people arriving on certain pages, and their interaction with your website, how much money was made. And that's pretty cool that you can track that inside of GetEmails, but right now, in this account, we're just using it to collect the leads, to collect the names, the emails, and the mailing address. As you can see here a whole bunch of contacts were collected. You can see that around the time of that launch in November we had a huge influx of contacts coming in. And those are all people who we can now email market to, and they're all collected here, in the downloadable contact's section. And what you used to have to do, depending on which plan you were on, was manually collect these people after a certain period of time.

Now it's all real-time and you can actually come over here to the integrations tab and you can actually integrate with your email marketing software your third-party apps or what have you, in order to automatically have the contact information sent to your various marketing platforms, as they come in, in real-time so very cool that you can do that now. So, you've got the dashboard, integration contact, the next thing you've got is the code snippet. The code snippet, now for the code snippet, this is pretty important. This is the most important aspect of this actually, this is where you're going to get the piece of code that you want to attach to your website. What you're going to do is you're going to come here to your scripts, pop up that comes up. And as you can see there's no code in there yet because you haven't specified what type of code it is. What you want to choose for collecting, is obviously collection, not suppression. Okay, suppression means don't give me contacts who have been on this page, whatever page you end up putting this snippet on. Okay, revenue tracking, like I said, is the more advanced thing where you're going to sort of get an impression of how much money you made, based on people landing on certain pages and so on and so forth. So, cool features we're not going to get into that right now. We're looking at the core aspect of GetEmails, and that is collecting emails of visitors. So, we're going to go with collection, what you would do is you would grab this code you'd copy it, and then you would go over to your web page, and you know depending on which content management system you're using. If you're using WordPress or Clickfunnels or Instapage it's going to be different, but it's actually going to be very similar. The whole concept, you've probably done this before, you've probably pasted scripts, like Google tag manager or your Facebook tracking pixel and so on and so forth. But basically, you've come over to wherever you do that in your platform, and you place it into the appropriate tracking scripts section, it doesn't actually specify here, which section to put it in. So, I'm assuming it doesn't matter too much.

The only difference here is the order in which things get loaded on your page and in this case, it doesn't actually matter too much. I don't think and so you can put it in the header section or in the body or in the footer section, you would paste that right here, and you want to make sure that it's not just generally on your website, we theoretically you could do that if you wanted to, but what you really want to do is focus on which page you're going after so that you can in your follow-ups, make references to the thing that the person was looking at. Right, and we'll talk about the importance of the very unique style of follow-ups that you're going to be sending in the next module, but that that makes it all the more important to try and use specificity with, a which pages you're attaching your script to, and then, you know, use specificity again with the emails that you're sending based on which pages they visited, and how, how you collected them. So for example let's say you've got a website and one part of your website you're selling, you know, drills and another part of your website, you're selling, glue, right, it's probably a good idea to set up a different snippet for each of those so that in your email, you can mention the fact that they checked out your website and we're interested in your glue and then you can have a live link in there that you can they can click on, which will allow you to, you know, measure their behavior and their interaction so on and so forth which we'll get into that in module three anyway. But specificity is good as I'm saying specificity is good. So having different ones for the different types of things that they might be interacting with on your web page is a good idea. But that's how you do that here. It's pretty simple, very simple, very similar to grabbing you know your fixed Facebook retargeting pixel, or your Google remarketing tags and so on and so forth.

So that's the code snippets suppression lists. That's basically where you tell them that someone who's on this page is someone who you do not want to collect, and the most clear example of this would be basically people who get to your thank you page after opting into your list, right. And let me explain the logic here. So, let's say you have a landing page or lead generation page where people can type in their email address, right. And then you have the thank you page or maybe it's a tripwire or an upsell page after that whatever it is the page that they get to only if they typed in their email address on the first page, right. If they get to that second page, that means that they already voluntarily gave you their email address. So, you don't want to get emails to grab their email, in this other unique method, right this unique approach to grabbing their emails, it's redundant and it can potentially cause problems.

And so, If, if they landed on that page, it means that you got their email address in the traditional way, so you don't need to collect it this way. Okay, or maybe you do want to, you might have your own reasons, but the general prevailing logic would be that if you're already collecting them, you only get a certain number of contacts per month that you're paying for, you don't want to waste that on people whose email addresses you already got because they did opt-in, you only want the people who didn't opt-in. Right, and so suppression lists are a way that you would do that.

Let's see your trends, just a way to analyze and track your data event detail. That's for enable revenue trafficking to track sales and ROI assets that has to do with the you know the actual more in-depth and complex tracking to see you know the effectiveness of your traffic and the revenue that you're generating, we talked about that already. And support, I know there's a throughout the manual mentality, among many people in the internet marketing space. But in this case, because it really is, it actually genuinely is a novel and unique and new concept, which is not something that happens very often in this space. This is an area where you actually do want to spend some time you do want to read through this, you do want to make sure you have a good understanding of how to do things and, you know the why and the what, you know. Make sure you're understanding this tool, because it is new and it's unique, that makes it all the more important but, that's basically a walkthrough of the GetEmails account area, and how to set it up on your landing page, the most important part of all of this, is how to follow up with these people because it has to be done very careful and unique way, it can't be done in the traditional marketing way, because they did not voluntarily as far as they're concerned, remember, legally speaking they did because they consent to something in the past, but they did not voluntarily and specifically opt-in to your list, in a way that they understand or remember. And so, you really have to be careful and deliberate and handleless in a unique way when you're sending your first email to them, and we'll talk about that in the next module.

Module 3

All right, welcome to module three. In this module, our expert will cover the unique follow-up campaigns you'll need, so get ready to take some notes, and let's jump right in.

Alright, so this is possibly the most important part of this training, the follow-up campaigns. These are going to be very, very unique and very different, they have to be, they have to be alright. And the reasons are obvious, because these people did not opt-in to your list, and therefore you cannot market to them. In the same way that you market to your regular subscriber list or customer list of people who have opted in or purchase things from you, you just can't. You're going to have ridiculous levels of spam and complaints and unsubscribes and things that are just going to destroy your deliverability. Right, which is why you should actually be using a separate autoresponder for this type of list your anonymous lead generation list should be in a different autoresponder and a different email domain, so that it doesn't impact your regular email marketing, right so you want some automation in place, that people come through that are very unique and we'll talk about that in a second. Right, but you want people to come through those automations via an email from, domain right, from address with a from email domain that is different from your regular email marketing. Right, and preferably an autoresponder, account, or a different autoresponder software altogether, that is different from your regular email marketing.

You want them to go through this sequence of marketing, very unique marketing, first, and then once they've ended the automation or the journey, in a way that you're satisfied with, then you can upgrade them to and then move them on to your main list based on their behavior. Right, so if they've opened your emails and clicked your links and interacted and so on and so forth. You know you can set up triggers that cause them to then, be added with an API integration, for example, let's say, or even something third party like Zapier, that can cause them to be added to your regular email marketing, but you've got to use this as a filter, and it has to be isolated so that doesn't bring down all of your regular email marketing.

So, why, does this have to be so different. Why is it such a big deal that your follow-up campaigns are so different from your regular email marketing follow-up campaigns, it's because they didn't opt-in, and a huge number of them are going to be angry or annoyed or confused. Right, it makes no sense, so obviously you can't say something clear like hey thanks for joining my list or thanks for requesting such and such, because they didn't, right. You can't say something like that, but also just the tone, such as the words, but the tone of the email needs to be very different. Okay, you need to say something in your first email to them. Right, your first unsolicited you got to keep that in mind, your first unsolicited email to them. You need to say something that sounds benign and natural, and logical enough, to fit the situation.

And I'll be honest, the easiest way to do that is a very short email that acknowledges that they visited your website. Okay, that's actually the easiest way to do this, it's the way that's going to probably get you the least amount of friction. Right, so let's say someone comes to your website let's say you sell, I don't know. Let's say you sell gas generators, right backup generators, and someone came to your website, and then they left, and you've got their email now, because of this special software. Right, what you would send is something very short and sweet, something along the lines of, because you're collecting their name here too, you could say, Bob, just wanted to say thanks for checking out our website today.

If you need more information on X Y Z generators. We have a great article over here, you know that you've got a link that they can click on. Right, you want something that they can click on to interact with because you want triggers you want to be able to filter based on their behavior that's really important. You know you want them to have an opportunity to interact because once they interact. That indicates that they are interested in your content, right, and you can use that as one of your triggers or your filters for who makes it through this whole process and onto your regular email list, your regular email marketing process. So, you want to make sure that you mentioned the fact that they, visited your website, and you're still just be advised, you're still going to get some friction, you're still going to get people saying wait a minute I didn't opt-in, they're going to remember, in many cases they're going to remember that they came to your website and that they did not opt-in, and they might send you a nasty gram they might get angry, they might unsubscribe they might hit the spam button, but if you keep it benign, you keep it really benign hey thanks for checking out our website today. Let me know if you have any questions, click here to book a call. We have a great article here or giving away a free, you know, XYZ. Just click here to grab it, right, and make that as frictionless as possible because you don't need them to opt-in, because you already have their email address so, you know, just have it, something that they can literally just grab, maybe even an attachment. You know something to earn a little bit of goodwill, keep it benign and simple, and pleasant. And that's going to be the best, best way to do this.

And I don't want to scare you too much, you're not probably going to have a huge, huge amount of people complaining, most people will probably just ignore the emails, that's what most people tend to do, but obviously, you're going to have a significantly higher rate of spam or complaints than you usually would on a regular email list obviously just makes logical sense. But many people are just going to ignore them, many people are going to open them, and they might give you know, five seconds of thought to the fact that wait a minute I didn't opt into anything I didn't subscribe, and then immediately, you know, ignore that, and move on and click on the link that you sent them.

And I'll be honest, a lot of people, and we're living in the age of email marketing and opt-ins and subscribing and stuff. A lot of people aren't even going to notice it. A lot of people won't remember that they didn't opt-in, they'll assume that they must have, they'll assume that they must have opted in, you know, and other explanations might exist. Oh, that that site probably had one of those, you know, log in with Facebook buttons or something along those lines, you know, there's so many ways that people are used to opting into things, you know, inadvertently or not necessarily inadvertently but in a way that was not directly, related to the action that they wanted to do. Those, you know, log in with Facebook API integrations are a perfect example of that, the rate at which people are used to just typing in their email address or actually the autofill feature on most people's laptops and desktops and mobile devices. You know where they just have a field and boom their email address pops up as an option and they tap that and they can, they can often so quickly, people are so used to doing that, in such a carefree and almost mindless manner, that in many cases they won't even realize that they didn't opt-in to your list, they won't even be conscious of it, they'll just assume that they did. And so the negative results aren't going to be terrible, I'm not trying to scare you with the whole idea that you know you're going to, you're going to get roasted by these people, but I do that the reason I'm stressing, the increased rate that you will see if complaints and spam and then, you know, nasty grams is simply to make it clear and drive home the point that you really want to keep this, isolated from your regular email marketing do not, I repeat do not integrate this directly to your regular email marketing software.

And so, the next question is how do you continue the conversation, how do you continue the conversation after the initial follow-up. Well, I would say the first couple of emails that you send in an automation sequence should all be the same, two or three emails should be the same as that first one, very benign, you know, very sort of nonchalantly acknowledging that they visited your website and then presenting them with something, a link to a blog post or something that they can click on so that you see their interaction with your emails or see whether or not they interacted at all.

And then you can sort of ease into some more traditional marketing from that point forward. Okay, because a lot of people, even if they didn't open your emails, or even if they, you know, looked at your emails and got angry or annoyed or confused after they've seen them two or three times floating around with the other, you know, 500 marketing emails that they get every day. It's just going to sort of naturally resolve itself, you know, and then you will be a name that they're used to seeing in their inbox, and if they don't like it, they'll unsubscribe. Right, so you can gradually after two or three very gentle and nonchalant and benign introductory emails, like the ones we mentioned, gradually ease them into some more traditional marketing, and then I would say, based on their behavior throughout your automation sequence based on whether they opened and whether they clicked and so on and so forth. Then set up some automation and some triggers, that will cause them to be moved over to your regular list to your main list, does that kind of make sense?

Now another follow-up question here because, with this software, you are, as we mentioned, able to get the physical mailing address, the postal address. And that's huge because postal addresses, or excuse me postage, marketing, marketing through physical mail, is a whole different ball game. You know it's more disconnected, it will just, by its nature, because it's physical mail it'll be, you know, days after they visited your site, you know, so they're more likely to not, remember they're more likely to not, you know, have to have a negative interpretation of receiving your message in the mail. And so you don't have to be as careful, you don't have to, you know, act like you're walking around on eggshells, with the physical mail, you know, if you want to you can send them a letter or a postcard that acknowledges that they visited your website if you want to, but I don't feel like the need is as necessary there, just because of the way that people think of and handle, you know, physical mail, which they probably categorize as junk mail, when it's promotional. And because the blowback is not as bad. You know there's no spam button that they can click on their physical mailbox that's going to negatively impact your email marketing, you know, or get your account shut down or get to know you're from address, you know the email domain of you from address. To lose cool points with the ESPs and so on and so forth, right.

So, physical mail you don't have to really be walking on eggshells, but still, put some thought into it and make sure that you know you're marketing to them logically fits the scenario that they're in, you know, the fact that you've anonymously, grabbed their, their physical mailing address, legally, but anonymously, based on a website, visit just keep that in mind when you're formulating the offer that you're sending them in the mail, and the wording that you're using and so on and so forth, but the really important thing is keep your email marketing, isolated, and make sure that those first few follow-ups are written in a benign nonchalant manner, very different from your traditional marketing, and then gradually ease them into your regular marketing, and make sure you take their behavior and their interactions into account when you're determining when and if to move them from that isolated situation into your regular email marketing software and automations.

Don't miss out!

Visit the website below and you can sign up to receive emails whenever B. Vincent publishes a new book. There's no charge and no obligation.

https://books2read.com/r/B-A-QWUO-FXLPB

BOOKS 2 READ

Connecting independent readers to independent writers.

Also by B. Vincent

Affiliate Marketing
Affiliate Marketing

Standalone
Affiliate Recruiting
Business Layoffs & Firings
Business and Entrepreneur Guide
Business Remote Workforce
Career Transition
Project Management
Precision Targeting
Professional Development
Strategic Planning
Imminent List Building

About the Publisher

Accepting manuscripts in the most categories. We love to help people get their words available to the world.

Revival Waves of Glory focus is to provide more options to be published. We do traditional paperbacks, hardcovers, audio books and ebooks all over the world. A traditional royalty-based publisher that offers self-publishing options, Revival Waves provides a very author friendly and transparent publishing process, with President Bill Vincent involved in the full process of your book. Send us your manuscript and we will contact you as soon as possible.

Contact: Bill Vincent at rwgpublishing@yahoo.com www.rwgpublishing.com